THE PRACTICAL STRATEGIES SERIES
IN GIFTED EDUCATION

series editors
FRANCES A. KARNES & KRISTEN R. STEPHENS

Language Arts for Gifted Learners

Lauren Miller and Emily Lubkert

Routledge
Taylor & Francis Group

NEW YORK AND LONDON

First published 2012 by Prufrock Press Inc.

Published 2021 by Routledge
605 Third Avenue, New York, NY 10017
2 Park Square, Milton Park, Abingdon, Oxon OX14 4RN

Routledge is an imprint of the Taylor & Francis Group, an informa business

ISBN 13: 978-1-59363-890-0 (pbk)

Contents

The Practical Strategies Series in Gifted Education offers teachers, counselors, administrators, parents, and other interested parties up-to-date instructional techniques and information on a variety of issues pertinent to the field of gifted education. Each guide addresses a focused topic and is written by an individual with authority on the issue. Several guides have been published. Among the titles are:

- *Acceleration Strategies for Teaching Gifted Learners*
- *Curriculum Compacting: An Easy Start to Differentiating for High-Potential Students*
- *Enrichment Opportunities for Gifted Learners*
- *Independent Study for Gifted Learners*
- *Motivating Gifted Learners*
- *Questioning Strategies for Teaching the Gifted*
- *Social & Emotional Teaching Strategies*

For a current listing of available guides within the series, please visit Prufrock Press at http://www.prufrock.com.

Language arts instruction offers teachers a wealth of opportunities to challenge and excite all students, including those who are academically or intellectually gifted. The four domains of language arts—reading, writing, speaking, and listening—allow students to deeply explore new ideas and express themselves in meaningful ways. However, our own experiences as students and then as teachers and mentors to beginning teachers have shown us that all too often, gifted students do not receive challenging and stimulating language arts instruction. What is more common is "independent" reading and writing during which students do not benefit from the type of teacher scaffolding that facilitates critical thinking. This situation does not arise because of unskilled or uncaring teachers. Sometimes, large class sizes or a restrictive curriculum makes it more difficult for teachers to differentiate their instruction and meet the needs of all students.

In this book, we strive to remedy this situation by offering teachers concrete instructional strategies for meeting the needs of gifted students in language arts. After reviewing some common characteristics of gifted language arts students as well as several special populations whose unique needs should also be considered, many concrete components of high-quality language arts instruction are described. You will discover ways to challenge and excite your gifted students through reading, writing, speaking, and listening activities. Of course, those categories are seldom mutually exclusive; for example, speaking must accompany listening if it is to be meaningful, and so often students make sense of what they have read by writing and talking about it. We acknowledge that there may be some overlap in the following chapters, or that a strategy in one chapter may also be relevant for another instructional area. We see this as one of the best parts about teaching and learning in language arts, and encourage teachers to make connections between ideas where applicable.

Characteristics of Gifted Language Arts Students

Students who display giftedness in language arts often possess what is termed *verbal talent*, which refers to an individual's capacity to employ and make meaning of language (Bailey, 1996). Although *talent* or *capacity* suggests a natural, inborn ability, which gifted students may in fact possess, verbally talented children may not necessarily become gifted language arts students without the active involvement of their parents and teacher. Modeling and scaffolding are essential supports for all students, including gifted students (Bailey, 1996).

General Characteristics

As educators know all too well, there are no hard and fast rules when it comes to students. They each come from unique backgrounds and have different talents, needs, and challenges. Gifted students are no exception to this rule. Each child who is gifted has unique abilities. Students who are gifted in language arts may display talent in multiple areas, such as mathematics, leadership, or the arts. On the other hand, their talents may be concentrated in one area of language arts. Other factors, such as a student's status as an English language learner, a home environment lacking in age-appropriate and stimulating printed material, the coexistence of a disability, or a child's prior experiences due to his or her membership in a particular cultural group or gender, can all influence the manifestation of his or her verbal talent. However, as teachers of gifted language arts students, it is helpful to be aware of some general characteristics of exceptional verbal aptitude.

Students who display talent in language arts typically have verbal abilities at least 2 years beyond their chronologic grade level (Dooley, 1993; Passow, 1996; Wood, 2008). These advanced skills can be in any of the language arts domains, although in the classroom setting it is often easiest to observe advanced skills in reading and writing. Like gifted learners in other areas, verbally gifted students typically display an ability to focus intense interest on a topic and may express exuberant curiosity about new ideas related to that topic (Passow, 1996). For the classroom teacher looking to identify verbally talented students, it may be helpful to consider children who read, write, listen, or speak eagerly and beyond grade-level expectations; who display a marked interest in words and language; who have vocabularies beyond their grade level; who can engage in highly complex verbal activities; who demonstrate the ability to manipulate words in advanced ways (e.g., puns); and who demonstrate creativity or imagination in verbal or written expression (Duke University Talent Identification Program, 2010; Passow, 1996). (See Appendix A for a more extensive list of characteristics of gifted students.)

Special Populations

English language learners. It may be more difficult for educators to recognize and serve gifted learners from underrepresented populations. English language learners (ELLs), for example, are often underrepresented in gifted classrooms. One issue in the identification of verbally gifted ELLs may be a mismatch between the mainstream expectations of the ways in which giftedness manifests itself in the classroom and the culture of these students.

For example, one common belief about gifted students, particularly in the language arts, is that they have large vocabularies. ELLs are in the process of acquiring a new language, which generally can take 5–7 years, even in an immersion setting. A verbally gifted ELL student may not have a large English vocabulary until he or she becomes extremely fluent in the English language. In most cases, ELLs do not have opportunities to display their native language vocabulary in the classroom. Even after they have reached a level of fluency in English, students may code-switch (move between languages in a single sentence or conversation), which can be perceived by teachers as indicating that they have not reached full mastery of the new language. However, because each language has unique words to express particular ideas, verbally gifted ELL students may code-switch to more accurately represent their thoughts. In this case, code-switching can indicate advanced skills in both the native and new languages, not a lack of mastery of either. Teachers must move beyond thinking about verbal giftedness simply in terms of vocabulary.

The use of humor, another common identifier of exceptional verbal aptitude, is far more complex to grasp in a second language and therefore may not be demonstrated in a classroom. Although some humor can be considered universal, much of it is cultural and therefore may not be accessible to a student who does not share the same culture. Verbally gifted ELL students may not "get" verbal humor used by teachers or classmates. They also may not use humor when writing or speaking in their second language.

Both regular education and gifted education teachers should use all available resources to help identify verbal talent in ELL students. Parental input can be helpful in the identification of gifted ELLs, possibly through completion of a behavioral checklist, as can the input of same-language peers, who may see gifted qualities not expressed in the classroom setting.

Culturally and socioeconomically diverse students. A well-documented achievement gap exists between the standardized test scores of White students and students of color as well as between poor students and their more affluent peers (Olszewski-Kubilius & Thomson, 2010). This gap extends into gifted programs, where poor and minority students are almost always underrepresented (Matthews & Shaunessy, 2008). Although this underrepresentation plagues school systems across the country, urban schools often have higher proportions of poor and/or minority students. Further compounding the problem for gifted students in urban schools is that these schools also tend to have a high percentage of struggling students, on whom the majority of resources are often focused because of pressures resulting from the current accountability environment (Bland, Coxon, Chandler, & VanTassel-Baska, 2010; Olszewski-Kubilius & Thomson, 2010). However, wherever socioeconomic and cultural diversity exist, teachers and school administrators should take care to ensure that all students are achieving at their highest potential.

Strategies to address underrepresentation of students of color as well as students from low-income backgrounds should target both identification and implementation. Because teacher referrals are often the first step in the identification process, teachers should familiarize themselves with the wide range of characteristics of gifted learners in order to broaden the scope of who might be considered gifted. In addition, teacher expectations can have a powerful effect on how students perform in school. Because of this, teachers should reflect on the assumptions they are making about students' potential for success and how those assumptions may affect instructional decisions, including how students are grouped (Ferguson, 2003; Rist, 1970). Finally, the identification process should include a wide range of measures beyond traditional IQ or achievement tests. Measures that focus on oral expressiveness, performance-based assessments, and nonverbal ability tests may increase the number of students identified as gifted in urban schools (Olszewski-Kubilius & Thomson, 2010).

Research suggests that these students do better in school when teachers focus on and build from their strengths, rather than fixating solely on weaknesses and deficits. However, students may need additional teacher scaffolding due to gaps in background knowledge or skills (Bland et al., 2010). For example, teachers may need to provide additional support in vocabulary acquisition or organizational skills in the form of modeling, guided practice, and many opportunities for student practice.

Students with special learning needs. One of the most difficult gifted populations to identify and serve appropriately is our students who are twice-exceptional. The vast diversity in the twice-exceptional population is part of what makes these students' identification so difficult. Gifted students in this category also have learning disabilities, physical disabilities, behavioral disorders, or psychological disorders. Their specific exceptionalities range from Asperger's syndrome, to ADHD, to hearing loss, to cerebral palsy.

In general, there are three categories of twice-exceptional students: those who are identified as both gifted and disabled, those who are identified in neither area (which in the case of learning disabilities can often be due to masking), and those who are identified in one area but not the other (King, 2005). Even when students are identified and served in both areas, there is often a discontinuity in their instruction that can cause dissonance and frustration to the student. King (2005) explained that students who are both gifted and learning disabled often feel frustrated that they cannot meet the expectations others have for their giftedness. This frustration can lead to dissatisfaction with school and low self-esteem. She noted that the most important task for teachers is to ensure that the gifted child receives instruction that challenges the area(s) of talent and helps remediate the child's area(s) of weakness.

Twice-exceptional students may need specific instruction in strategies for school success. Communication between all personnel that work with the student is vital, especially if the student has an Individualized Education Program (IEP; Weinfeld, Barnes-

Robinson, Jeweler, & Shevitz, 2005). One tip for teachers working to identify twice-exceptional students is to rely on parent information. Although twice-exceptional children sometimes feel they aren't "good" at school, they may demonstrate their gifts more freely at home (King, 2005). A teacher who listens carefully to parents may learn that a student reluctant to write more than a paragraph at school writes entire novels at home. Teachers must use all resources available to identify and serve students who may be twice-exceptional.

Gender differences. Gifted girls and boys share many of the same general characteristics. In addition, as with any category of students, teachers should remember that considerable variation exists within either gender group. However, it is worth noting that although early childhood and elementary gifted programs have similar numbers of boys and girls, the percentage of girls in gifted programs and advanced courses decreases as children get older. Gifted girls have several unique characteristics that can present special challenges to the adults who work with them. Most notably, they tend to be intellectually and verbally advanced but they may also be underachieving. Gifted girls often fear being too successful, believing that they will be rejected socially (especially by members of the opposite sex) if they appear too successful in school. This fear can lead them to hide or "mask" their giftedness, which can result in underachievement and/or a mismatch between their needs and their teachers' instructional practices (Manning & Besnoy, 2008).

Although gifted girls and young women are more likely to be underachieving, their underachievement may go beyond lower than expected performance in school. Gifted girls and young women face what might be termed cultural underachievement, which describes the depressed ambitions and goals of many young women. At young ages, gifted girls start out in a similar track as gifted boys. By adulthood, women are underrepresented in high-status jobs and underpaid when compared to male counterparts. As girls get older, they tend to become less confident and less likely to take academic/intellectual risks. This loss of confidence can inhibit their progress, leaving them less able to perform at high levels (Reis, 1987).

Teachers of early grades can focus on creating a conducive environment for success by encouraging girls to take risks and accept leadership roles in the classroom. Teachers should also limit traditional gender-role grouping and stereotyping. For example, teachers can encourage both boys and girls to choose literature based on their own interests as opposed to basing recommendations on gendered assumptions. In addition, teachers can introduce female role models, both past and present, on a frequent and consistent basis.

In older grades, the focus should also include interventions and counseling for gifted girls. If girls already suffer from a weakened self-concept, teachers can counsel and mentor girls to help them see themselves in a more positive light. In addition, teachers can encourage positive peer interactions between gifted girls to lessen the sense of isolation that many gifted girls feel. Finally, gifted girls should be encouraged to pursue advanced coursework in all subject areas.

Teaching Reading to Gifted Language Arts Students

Reading receives an enormous amount of attention in the primary years, when students are learning the actual decoding and comprehension skills that allow them to make meaning out of the printed word. However, as students get older, reading becomes a more nuanced task, and it can become more difficult for teachers to continue to challenge gifted readers. As former primary teachers, both authors have seen firsthand how difficult it is to differentiate for the advanced reader in the early grades. This challenge does not diminish as a student ages and becomes a more efficient and fluent reader.

Who Are Gifted Readers?

Catron and Wingenbach (1986) astutely observed that, "gifted readers go beyond learning to read and, instead, *read to learn*" (p. 135). This distinction is one of the most telling differences between good readers and talented readers. Even at an early age, a gifted reader understands the power of the written word and uses it to satisfy his curiosity about the world around him. Gifted readers may display advanced mastery of language, possess advanced language processing skills, and typically are avid readers (Reis et al., 2004). Although gifted readers may already take delight in the written word, teachers need to attend to their reading needs if we are to ensure that they become readers for life.

What Do Gifted Readers Need?

It is a sad reality that the instructional needs of gifted readers are often overlooked in the classroom. Many well-meaning teachers may feel that because gifted readers already know how to read, they should devote one-on-one instructional time to struggling or developing readers. As a result, one usually sees the teacher working intently with small groups of struggling to average readers during reading instruction, with a small scattering of gifted readers going the entire reading block without interacting with the teacher. These talented students may spend the 60–90-minute block of time reading independently, reading to struggling peers, plugged into a computer, or even working on other subject matter. This is not the kind of reading instruction gifted readers need or deserve.

Gifted readers need scaffolding at their instructional level. Because they developed reading skills at an earlier age than average readers, they may have learned to read outside the setting of the classroom. Consequently, there may be gaps between their ability to read and the skill set required to read at a more complex level. The most vital thing a classroom teacher can do for a gifted reader is to spend time carefully assessing the student's reading skills and noting the student's strengths and weaknesses. One of the authors, a voracious and early reader herself, vividly remembers her kindergarten teacher spending individual time reading early chapter books with her during the daily naptime. She developed a love for fiction and storytelling at an early age that has been sustained through adulthood. It is impossible to say whether she would have retained her appetite for reading without such early encouragement, but it is certain that it played a role in sustaining her passion for the written word.

Whereas reading in schools is typically taught in a bottom-up fashion, beginning with letters and sounds, gifted readers often approach reading in a top-down fashion, making frequent connections to the text and applying what they read to other areas of their lives (Catron & Wingenbach, 1986). A teacher of gifted readers will consequently need to ensure that her students are receiving instruction in higher order thinking skills, thinking metacognitively, and making connections to texts. Although all students should engage in these activities during reading time, gifted readers should be engaged almost exclusively in these activities rather than practicing decoding, summarizing, and remembering plot details.

Instructional Strategies

Grouping. One of the most challenging aspects of instructing talented readers is figuring out how to group them. We know that gifted learners need opportunities to interact with like-ability peers. It is essential that teachers remain flexible about the grouping of their students and keep in mind that the needs of their learners are more important than convenience.

At a large school, it may be entirely possible to maintain heterogeneous classrooms while still giving gifted readers opportunities to work with their gifted peers. Grade-level teams may be able to work out a rotation schedule whereby they cluster groups of gifted learners in a classroom or two for a period of time each day. The classroom during that period may remain multilevel or, if the school has a large number of gifted learners, the classroom may become more homogeneous. In either circumstance, the teacher working with these students will be able to group like-ability readers together, which will allow them to engage in reading activities at their ability level. One of the authors has used this approach before and has found that although there may be initial resistance from staff members and parents, dissent quickly disappears once all parties realize how beneficial the structure is for the students.

In a smaller school or a school with a smaller population of gifted readers, teachers may need to get more creative. Multigrade groupings may be necessary, which would require schedule alignment. Students in the upper grade levels of a school may need to be provided with transportation to a local middle school, high school, or college campus. A teacher or group of students from several grade levels may need to create a lunch bunch where they can engage in discussions of literature or dramatizations of texts they have read or share recommended readings with each other.

Read aloud. Because gifted readers are capable of reading texts beyond their chronological age, many adults assume they are more interested in reading a book themselves than listening to it read aloud. However, read-aloud is a strategy that both teachers and parents can use to engage students in more challenging literature, demonstrate how to choose a book, model problem-solving strategies in reading, and encourage higher level thinking. Another positive aspect of incorporating read-aloud in the regular education classroom is that a teacher can read aloud a book at the reading level of gifted learners and still engage the other students in the classroom. By asking different levels of questions, a teacher can easily differentiate for varying levels of learners. Plus, many students really love to be read to; unfortunately, read-aloud tends to be put away for independent reading time in upper elementary grades and beyond. However, students of many ages will listen raptly to thoughtfully chosen teacher read-alouds. Making time for them in your classroom is a good way to engage all learners.

Three types of reading. In order to engage talented students in reading suited to their abilities, teachers must plan deliberately to include different types of reading activities in their teaching. Catron and Wingenbach (1986) identified three types of reading that meet the cognitive and social-emotional needs of gifted learners: critical reading, creative reading, and inquiry reading.

Critical reading involves the careful selection and reading of books in order to draw particular meaning from the text.

Students or teachers may select fiction or nonfiction materials based around themes, styles, subjects, and so forth. Teachers engage students in drawing inferences, interpreting meaning, making predictions, and evaluating the worth of the written texts. This type of reading will develop these critical thinking skills in students, which students can then use on their own and in other subject areas.

Creative reading involves students in making their own meaning of a text. Students use synthesis, application, and extension skills in the creation of their own products related to a text. In early grades, this may consist of acting out a story, drawing a representation of a book's themes, or rewriting an ending. In later years, students could rewrite a text from a different character's point of view or in a different historical setting, create their own text in a similar style, or alter a text based on the absence or addition of a new event.

The final approach to reading, inquiry reading, involves students in reading to learn about a new topic or idea. Because gifted students already read to learn, this style of reading may come naturally to them. However, a teacher can scaffold students' learning by teaching them how to organize the new knowledge while modeling the practices of inquiry and providing age-appropriate materials. This type of reading empowers gifted students because they amass the skills necessary to do independent research on topics of interest.

Reading workshop. In our experience, writing workshop is used more often in classrooms than reading workshop. However, reading workshop is a valuable way to structure reading instruction, especially in classrooms where teachers have a fair amount of curricular freedom. The basic reading workshop structure begins with a short mini-lesson in which the teacher explains and models a particular reading strategy or skill, such as determining an author's purpose, examining literary techniques like personification, or making connections to personal experiences. The main work of reading workshop occurs in the next block, where students read independently. They may keep individual reading journals where they respond to specific or open-ended prompts about their reading. During this time, the teacher conferences one-on-one with students. As a final wrap-up to reading workshop, the class returns to a whole-group setting, and students share how they applied the strategy from the mini-lesson to their independent reading for the day. There are many variations on this basic structure that can be used to enhance reading workshop in your particular setting.

Several aspects of reading workshop make it appropriate for use with gifted readers. A strategy mini-lesson is a wonderful way to ensure that gifted readers don't miss out on specific, skill-based reading instruction. Often strategies can be differentiated so that students at different levels can see how the strategy can be applied to their reading. For example, in a mini-lesson on dialogue, a teacher could model reading dialogue and using context clues to determine which character is speaking. The majority of the readers in a classroom could apply the strategy in this manner. But in the same mini-lesson, the teacher could also show students how to examine clues that indicate the tone of the dialogue and how to use that tone to determine the characters' emotions or personalities. The gifted readers in the classroom could apply the strategy in this manner.

The individual conferencing aspect of reading workshop also helps meet the needs of gifted readers. As mentioned earlier, gifted readers are typically self-taught and may not have learned specific reading skills or strategies. Conferencing gives the teacher a chance to observe a gifted reader's areas of strength and weakness. Conferencing may help the teacher learn where to remediate or extend instruction for that particular student.

Literature circles/book clubs. Depending on the number of gifted learners in a classroom, literature circles can be integrated into the reading block in the regular education classroom, or can be formed outside of the classroom, whether during lunch, a free period, or before or after school. This effort may involve the teacher giving his or her time outside the school day, but this time will be well spent for the teacher who truly wants to mold students into lifelong readers. If teachers have access to a curriculum that utilizes a literature circle model, such as Junior Great Books, they may be able to use it with the whole class. (Another literature circle format, the Paideia Seminar, is profiled in Appendix B.) Many teachers split the class into two or three discussion groups during a Junior Great Books program because they want all students to have an opportunity to engage in the discussion. We advise frequently modifying groups so that gifted learners have an opportunity to engage with like-ability peers often.

The aspect of literature circles that benefits gifted readers is the opportunity to engage with like-ability peers in discussion about a text that every member in the group is reading. The discussion should be directed by students as much as possible, but should also engage them in critical thinking about the text. With younger or less experienced students, the teacher may need to facilitate discussion for the first few meetings. Questioning should be open-ended and lie at the higher levels of Bloom's taxonomy. The group may need to set norms for behavior, as rich discussion can only be had if all members of the group feel comfortable expressing their honest thoughts and opinions. As students become comfortable with the format, the teacher should turn much of the control of the group over to the students themselves.

Concept-based learning. Gifted students who are top-down learners often have the ability to consider a big picture and make connections between disciplines. Because of this, learning becomes more meaningful when a teacher uses concepts to tie together learning across curricular areas. A concept is a big idea that resonates with all people due to its fundamental nature in human existence. Some examples of concepts include conflict, interdependence, systems, and wisdom. A teacher can use a concept in a single unit or can use a single concept for an entire year. Because concepts are abstract and inherently meaningful in students' lives, an infinite number of connections can be made to a single concept.

The use of concepts helps students make connections to what they are learning both within and outside of the classroom. It is easy to see how a fifth-grade class of students who are using the concept of time as a lens will connect generalizations about time to their study of American history, weather and climate, graphing, and a novel study of *Island of the Blue Dolphins*. At the same time, students may connect the concept of time to their relationships with family members and friends, their extracurricular activities such as sports or music lessons, and their interests or hobbies. The use of concepts requires the teacher to plan lessons more deliberately, but will result in extended student learning. (See Appendix C for an example of a concept-based lesson.)

Teaching Writing to Gifted Language Arts Students

The writing process has often been characterized as a linear, tidy progression that begins with planning and ends with editing. However, in reality, writing is a much messier process during which writers are constantly planning, making decisions, and/or analyzing their work as it unfolds. By conceptualizing writing as a method of thinking and by implementing a wide range of writing activities, teachers can facilitate students' ability to understand any subject. Critical thinking skills such as synthesis and evaluation, often encouraged in gifted students, can be practiced and developed through writing. Teachers can capitalize on students' talents for verbal expression by enhancing their creativity and critical thinking skills along with their writing ability.

Who Are Gifted Writers?

Gifted writers have often demonstrated earlier signs of being verbally talented, such as being orally expressive or learning to read at an early age, before they learn to write (Bailey, 1996). However, writing has some special features that may delay its appearance. First, like reading, writing requires a higher level of abstraction than speaking, where meaning is conveyed directly through speech. When students read and write, they must make meaning of ideas by deciphering a written code. In addition, the development of fine motor skills is a prerequisite to learning to write, and so even highly verbally talented children must "wait" until their bodies catch up to their minds (Bailey, 1996).

However, when young gifted students do begin to write, it may appear, as in one case study of a gifted writer, that the new opportunity to write "provides a spigot for [their] verbal talent" (Bailey, 1996, p. 106). Gifted students often enjoy the freedom and creativity afforded to them during writing time. In addition, writing may offer gifted students the chance to exercise other general learning strengths, such as the ability to work strategically and independently as well as the ability to monitor their own progress on a task (Schunk & Swartz, 1993). This is especially likely when writing instruction focuses on the writing process and when teachers give students opportunities for independence and choice.

Piirto (1992) identified 16 capacities demonstrated in the writing of highly gifted writers, which included the uses of paradox, rhythm, and visual imagery as well as a sense of humor, the ability to play with language, and the inclusion of a moral or philosophical perspective. Although Piirto's research focused on child prodigies (i.e., highly gifted children whose writing abilities match those of an adult), less exceptionally gifted students may still exhibit some of these qualities. In addition, the ability of a young student to employ symbolism in writing, indicating abstract thought, may signal that he or she is a gifted writer (Bailey, 1996).

Teachers should keep in mind that gifted students are often characterized by asynchronous development, which means that their performance in different areas may appear uneven (Reis & Housand, 2008). Common characteristics of gifted students may not necessarily translate into writing ability. For example, children with large vocabularies may not be able to put the full extent of their word knowledge to use in their own writing (Master, 1983).

What Do Gifted Writers Need?

Just as gifted readers should not be left to read independently for the entirety of their classroom's reading block, neither should gifted students be expected to learn writing skills on their own. Gifted students still need to learn foundational skills, like sentence and paragraph construction. Although their skills may be more advanced than those of their peers, it is unlikely that an elementary-age student will have already mastered the full extent of skills necessary for coherent written expression. Students may need explicit instruction, modeling, and opportunities to practice new skills in a meaningful context (Master, 1983).

Most importantly, students need the opportunity to develop their talents with frequent opportunities to write in different modes, with different target audiences, and for varying purposes (Bailey, 1996). Students will be enthusiastic and eager writers when they are given regular opportunities to write for authentic purposes that incorporate their own motivations to write. Overly prescriptive writing prompts that have no real audience (besides the teacher who will read the piece only to grade it) will not hold a gifted writer's attention for long.

Instructional Strategies

Writing workshop. In writing workshop, writing is envisioned as a process of planning, drafting, revising, editing, and occasionally publishing. As in reading workshop, the teacher presents strategies for good practice through daily mini-lessons, where he or she models how to apply a particular strategy. Writing mini-lessons typically include the use of high-quality literature as models, so that students can link what they are doing in the classroom to "real" writing. For example, a first-grade teacher could use *A Chair for My Mother* by Vera B. Williams to demonstrate how an author includes lots of detail about a short period of time. After the mini-lesson, students write independently while the teacher conferences with individual students. Independent writing also gives the teacher an opportunity to assemble a group of students for additional instruction or modeling. At the end of writing workshop, the students gather together to share some examples of their work with an emphasis on discussing how they used the strategy discussed in the mini-lesson.

Some of the benefits of reading workshop, as described previously, also apply to writing instruction. The extended time devoted to independent writing gives teachers the time and space to differentiate. For example, a teacher could use an individual conference or small-group meeting to expand on the mini-lesson and model a more nuanced or advanced use of the target strategy for gifted writers. In addition, mini-lessons provide consistent strategy instruction, which is valuable for all learners. Over time, students develop the ability to "take what they need" from the skills and strategies modeled by the teacher, resulting in an ever-expanding toolbox of writing skills (Graves, 1983, p. 50).

The process approach. In writing workshop, teachers typically use the process approach to writing. In contrast to the more traditional product approach, in which most of the teacher's attention is focused on evaluating the final written product, the process approach emphasizes the different steps that all writers go through when composing a piece (Graves, 1983). These steps may be called by different names, depending on the specific version of the process approach that is being used, but they can be generalized as prewriting, writing, and rewriting (Collins & Parkhurst, 1996). Students focus more time on developing their ideas and expressing them to an audience and less time on mechanics and grammar. This is not to say that the process approach ignores mechanics; however, it does elevate the writer's purpose and frames mechanics as a means toward the end of communicating a message (Kennedy, 1996).

Gifted language arts students will benefit from the process approach for several reasons. First, most teachers agree that all students, including gifted students, need support and scaffolding at their instructional level as they learn to write (Graves, 1983). In addition, the process approach allows students a greater degree of freedom as they choose and explore a topic. This independence and active involvement in their own learning is highly valued by many gifted students (Armstrong, 1994). Third, gifted learners can become overwhelmed with ideas when trying to choose a topic for writing. Prewriting activities, like free writing or idea webbing, allow gifted students to devote time to brainstorming. When gifted students do not have to rush to pick the "best" idea, their feelings of being overwhelmed may recede. In addition, in our experience, using the process approach helps the work of writing become more meaningful to students. The time spent choosing a topic, developing one's ideas, and revising one's work represents a significant investment of time during which students become very connected to their writing. Finally, the process approach's inclusion of revision and rewriting may help students to overcome perfectionism, which can paralyze gifted students who are used to constant success in school (Collins & Parkhurst, 1996).

Three types of writing. It is imperative that gifted learners have many opportunities to write in a variety of different modes, with different purposes, and to different audiences. This kind of writing instruction "force[s] students to operate at the edge rather than at the center of their abilities" (Bailey, 1996, p. 110). It is only when we challenge our gifted learners that they will continue to learn and develop.

There are three main types of writing that students should learn and practice: expressive, transactional, and poetic (Collins & Parkhurst, 1996). Expressive writing is typically where beginning writers start, and it is usually the easiest kind of writing because it is the closest to oral expression. The most common occurrence of expressive writing in schools is journal entries and personal letters, which can serve as opportunities for students to gain confidence as they learn to write. As students become more adept at expressing themselves through writing, teachers can move onto transactional and poetic language. Transactional writing, also known as expository writing, is writing intended to do something: persuade the reader, summarize an event, or record research. Although transactional writing can be very impersonal and unconnected from students' lives, it can become more relevant when students get to select their own topics and create meaningful work through the process approach. When working with a relevant topic, gifted students often thrive with a transactional writing assignment because it gives them a chance to share some of their extensive knowledge on a topic.

The third category of writing is poetic writing, which goes beyond rhyming poetry and more broadly describes writing that is used to "create rather than accomplish" (Collins & Parkhurst, 1996, p. 278). Creative and verbally talented students will love the chance to exercise their strengths, use their imaginations, and play with words in interesting ways. Poems, stories, plays, and songs are all examples of poetic writing.

Literature and Language for Gifted Language Arts Students

Many teachers we have met are concerned about finding literature to suit gifted readers. Because gifted readers are typically able to read materials that are designed for children of an older chronological age, teachers and parents worry that books at a gifted reader's level will contain content that is not age appropriate. The increased availability of and interest in web-based media aimed at both children and adults further complicates decisions about what literature to use with gifted readers. Because we can't preview every piece of reading material available to students, one of our major roles as teachers is to teach our students how to evaluate and select literature that is both age-appropriate and appropriately challenging.

What Types of Literature Should Gifted Language Arts Students Read?

Gifted readers are diverse, and there is no single type of book or genre they should read. However, there are some ideas teachers may wish to take into consideration when guiding gifted readers toward literature. Patricia Austin (2003), a children's book author, offered several tips for choosing books for gifted readers. She noted that reading selections should have "rich, precise, and varied language"; a nontraditional structure (e.g., nonlinear time structure or narration from multiple points of view); characters who could be seen as role models; or characters who present potential career fields for gifted learners. Obviously most books will not have all of these categories, but teachers can look to stock their classroom library with a variety of books that meet these criteria.

Thompson (1996b) made a strong argument for the use of the "classics" with gifted readers. By classics, he meant both ancient and contemporary literature that has remained timeless and includes varied authors such as Shakespeare, Victor Hugo, and Harper Lee. He gave several reasons why the classics can be powerful tools in the instruction of gifted readers, including their inherent ability to self-differentiate; their ability to expose students to a rich, advanced vocabulary; their use of powerful, universal themes; and their power to develop thinking skills.

Literature can be used to address the social and emotional needs of gifted students. This approach, commonly known as bibliotherapy, matches some aspect of the text's content to the affective needs of the reader. Literature may be matched with a reader because the student is dealing with a challenge similar to that of the main character (e.g., feeling different because of his or her gifts and talents). In order to match texts to a student's needs, teachers will need to be attuned to the student's development. It can be helpful to include texts that match a student's need in a browsing box so the student does not feel singled out by the teacher or forced to read a particular text.

Many teachers assume that gifted readers will automatically seek out a variety of genres because of their intense interest in the written word. This is usually not so, and in fact, talented readers can often get "stuck" in a particular genre or theme because of their intensity. Teachers must deliberately provide students with opportunities to engage in a variety of genres, including, but not limited to, fiction, poetry, biographies, informational media such as newspapers and magazines, mythology, and various other forms of nonfiction. Read-alouds are a wonderful way to model interest in a variety of genres and to introduce gifted readers to genres they display reluctance toward. Access to online media such as news sites, blogs, and discussion forums may be important for older gifted readers. However, like print media, teachers should monitor online media carefully. Because these materials change more rapidly than printed text, the monitoring process should be more frequent. Teachers who wish to use approved online media sites in their classrooms may consider partnering with the school librarian or other interested teachers to share the monitoring duties.

How Can Teachers Ensure Their Students Have Access to High-Quality Literature?

In the past several decades, there has been a back-and-forth battle over the use of basal readers in lieu of literature, especially in early elementary classrooms. If a basal system is in place in the school district in which you teach, there are several steps you can take to ensure that your students still have access to a variety of engaging and challenging literature.

A classroom that emphasizes reading as an important part of learning should have plenty of actual books available to students. Each day, students need to have access to these books and should have opportunities to read individually and to hear books read aloud by the teacher or peers. Children also need opportunities to reflect on and share their ideas about these books, either in writing, in small discussion groups, or one-on-one with the teacher.

One strategy for teachers without access to a large classroom library is to use either the public library or the Internet. Many public libraries will allow teachers extended access to books, although unless a teacher feels entirely confident in their students' responsibility, it may be better to keep the books in the classroom rather than send them home with the students. The Internet also has a number of high-quality sites that offer virtual reading of books in their original form (see http://www.storylineonline.net or http://us.penguingroup.com/static/pages/publishersoffice/screeningroom). Yard sales and seasonal library sales, where libraries sell unneeded book donations at a low cost, from 50¢ to $1 per book, can be a great place for teachers to amass classroom library materials at a lower cost.

How Can Teachers Extend the Study of Language for Gifted Learners?

Thompson (1996a) noted that specific instruction in language is an oft-ignored topic in the literature about gifted language arts students. He argued that language is the manner in which individuals express their thoughts and, therefore, the study of language is an absolutely vital part of instruction of verbally gifted students. Gifted language arts students have advanced knowledge of and interest in language; it seems obvious that they need instruction in this topic at school. In addition, as Thompson (1996a) shared, language is complex, abstract, interdisciplinary, and higher order; all of these qualities are important parts of instruction for gifted language arts students. Thompson (1996a) argued that students should receive instruction in three areas of language study, including grammar, vocabulary, and poetics. Grammar, however, does not have to be taught in the dry manner typical in most classrooms, but can be used as a tool for analyzing an author's word choices and their meanings. Vocabulary can come alive through etymology, the study of words' Greek and Latin roots. Poetics, in this case, is the study of how language choices impart meaning and tone. Gifted students also deserve opportunities to engage in word play through analogies, riddles, anagrams, and poetry. They should engage with verbal humor, both through analysis of the humor of others and through the creation and use of their own humor.

Language Arts in the Content Areas

Language arts instruction is easily extended into many subject areas, as reading, writing, and speaking are the main ways that students take in new ideas, process information, and express their own understandings. If you choose to implement concept-based learning, as described previously, you will naturally integrate language arts into other subject areas as you plan your instruction. By infusing language arts instruction into the entire school day, you will meet the needs of gifted learners who thrive on making connections between different elements and are able to see the "big picture" of conceptual understanding.

Instructional Strategies

Interdisciplinary reading. Talented readers make meaningful connections, and they do so easily. These connections can be to personal experience or to prior knowledge. They can also be to other subject areas. Teachers of gifted readers should provide structured opportunities for students to do interdisciplinary reading. If the class is studying a science, math, or social studies topic that particularly interests a gifted reader, the teacher could provide that student with an independent study opportunity that allows him or her to explore that interest during reading time. The same could be done with an outside passion of the student, perhaps in ballet, dinosaurs, or the environment. Another bonus of interdisciplinary reading is that it frequently provides opportunities for the student to read a variety of genres or types of writing, which enhances reading skills.

Writing in the content areas. Writing activities can be used in every subject area, helping students achieve at least two goals: increased understanding of a topic and improved writing skills. Infusing writing into other content areas offers teachers and students many benefits. First, writing can stimulate learning, because as students write about a topic, they process their thoughts about it, make new connections to it, and deepen their understanding of the topic. An example of a "writing-to-learn" activity is microthemes, where students respond to a question on a note card. The size limitation forces students to distill their thoughts and focus on what is most important about a topic.

In addition, writing can facilitate metacognition, an important skill for planning and self-regulation. Writing activities can help students "think about their thinking" by forcing them to stop and reflect on what they were doing or thinking about. Metacognitive writing activities encourage students to thoughtfully consider their mental processes. For example, at the end of a math lesson, students can quickly respond to some or all of the following prompts:

- Write about what you did in class today.
- What did you learn?
- What are you unsure about, confused by, or wondering about?
- Describe what was easy and what was hard for you.

These prompts will help students process the mathematical thinking that they have just completed and lead them to develop questions and goals for the next lesson. By putting students in touch with their own thinking and learning, metacognitive writing activities grant gifted students the active involvement, control, and independence that they often desire (Armstrong, 1994). Finally, student writing can be an excellent source of formative assessment data. Writing provides a record of where students are in their learning and can expose misconceptions as well as identify understandings. (See Appendix D for additional writing activities.)

Writing in the content areas, also known as writing across the curriculum (WAC), does not necessarily conflict with the process approach to writing, as discussed previously. For example, the microtheme activity described above can be used as a prewriting activity as students prepare to write a longer paper about a topic (Kennedy, 1996). Also, as students take notes while researching a topic, the teacher can prompt them to think about how the text is organized and why they think the author made that choice. These reflections will stimulate thinking about students' own writing.

Parallel curriculum. The Parallel Curriculum Model (PCM; Tomlinson et al., 2002) is similar to concept-based learning in that teachers take a holistic approach to a topic, with students developing a fuller understanding of how different ideas connect to each other. PCM has four components and each has a specific goal or purpose:

- *Core Curriculum:* the learning objectives and curriculum frameworks that guide the content of an entire unit;
- *Curriculum of Connections:* where students link ideas across time, space, and culture;
- *Curriculum of Practice:* activities designed to actively involve students in the content as practitioners (e.g., historians, mathematicians, scientists); and
- *Curriculum of Identity:* opportunities for students to reflect on their own senses of self and how they relate to the important ideas and behaviors of a field.

These four components provide many opportunities to differentiate instruction to meet the needs of all learners, including gifted students. Language arts instruction is a key piece of PCM because of the multiple ways that students make meaning of a topic. Reading, writing, and speaking are the gateways to the full range of meaning-making that PCM entails. (See Purcell, Burns, & Leppien, 2002, for an excellent example of PCM.)

Oral Communication for Gifted Language Arts Students

Oral communication can be conceptualized as "thinking in action" (Chaney, 1996, p. 115). Although we know that verbal abilities consist of reading, writing, listening, and speaking, the latter two skill sets typically receive very little direct instruction in school. Many experts believe that overlooking the importance of listening and speaking limits students' verbal growth, especially amongst gifted students who may become leaders in their fields and will require the ability to inform or persuade their constituents. Luckily, there are many strategies teachers can incorporate into their language arts instruction that will build oral communication skills in their students.

Instructional Strategies

Foreign language instruction. Verbally gifted learners demonstrate advanced mastery of their own language. They rarely have to attend carefully to the speech of others in order to understand what they are saying. They speak easily and often without extensive thought because words come easily to them. Learning a new language places students back into a situation in which they have to attend very carefully to the spoken word (Cramond, 1993). Consequently, it is a great way to help students develop their listening and speaking skills. Foreign language instruction will also help gifted students learn about cultures other than their own, practice perspective taking, and provide them with a skill that will benefit them later in life. Gifted learners, who are intensely curious about language, may love learning a new language and consequently may find a new academic passion through the study of a foreign language.

Debate. Debate is not a typical learning activity in most American classrooms, where many teachers favor lecture and drill-and-practice activities. The lack of debate may also stem from teachers' discomfort with discord and their sensitivity to the varied backgrounds and points of view of their learners. However, debate builds critical thinking skills, the ability to thoughtfully respond, and critical listening in students (Cramond, 1993). When a teacher carefully teaches debate as a series of actions, including examining an issue from all sides, presenting a position in a rational manner, listening carefully to the positions of others, and graciously accepting the end result of the debate, it builds important skills in students (Cramond, 1993). The abilities to listen, reason, and accept the positions of others are inherently useful in real life. Teachers can use debate in the study of literature, asking students to take the side of a particular character or individual from a fiction or nonfiction book. After teachers have become comfortable with the idea of disagreement among students and students have become comfortable with a lack of resolution, the class can move to more complex or contentious debate issues, such as those that might be situated in social studies or history.

Drama. Like debate, the use of drama in classrooms builds skills that students will find useful in life. Drama builds students' speaking skills, particularly their ability to speak to an audience. The ability to speak clearly and confidently in front of a crowd, to persuade others, and to express oneself are all important skills that can be built through drama. Playwriting and acting also allow for creativity and personal expression (Cramond, 1993). Although many children naturally tend toward dramatic play in their early years, if they are discouraged in this type of play, they may become less comfortable with dramatic activities. By integrating drama into early elementary lessons, whether through reader's theater, class plays, playwriting, or dramatic play, teachers can validate these forms of learning as appropriate within the classroom and can help students build a foundation for these types of activities later in life.

Evaluative listening. Chaney (1996) noted that much of oral communication is persuasive. Whether students are deciding what game to play with their friends on the playground, negotiating how many vegetables they have to eat at dinnertime, or executing an instruction from a teacher or coach, they are evaluating information they are given and making decisions about whether and how to accept that information. Listening is a vital part of an individual's daily life, but it is often assumed that it is a self-taught skill. Teachers can use instructive listening practice in their classrooms, which Chaney (1996) called evaluative listening. In evaluative listening, students are taught to listen to all parts of an argument and consider those parts as they formulate a response to the argument. This type of activity could be embedded in other content areas of the curriculum (e.g., listening to Martin Luther King Jr.'s "I Have a Dream" speech during a study of the American Civil Rights Movement). Students could also integrate listening activities into their independent studies (e.g., listening to and evaluating the arguments of a variety of sources during a study of climate change).

Interviewing. Cramond (1993) noted that interviewing is an oral communication activity that satisfies curiosity, builds the ability to formulate and ask questions, listen critically, and synthesize. Gifted students, with their natural curiosity and verbal precocity, may respond positively to interviewing activities throughout their schooling. Teachers can build interviewing into the curriculum in a variety of authentic and creative ways. At a basic level, teachers can ask students to conduct interviews of family or community members during appropriate units on American history or personal culture. When studying historical figures who are no longer alive, the teacher could assign a mock interview between pairs of students in which one student has to imagine he or she is the historical figure and the other student is the interviewer. Written products from these interviews can always be incorporated into writing instruction in the classroom. If students respond well to interview assignments, a teacher could create a class or school newspaper for which students could conduct frequent interviews. This project would appeal to gifted students' desires to create authentic products.

Extending the Curriculum for Gifted Language Arts Students

One of the greatest challenges facing educators today is meeting the highly diverse needs of every student. In nearly every classroom, children of different backgrounds have different strengths, weaknesses, interests, and abilities, and teachers are responsible for making sure that every student reaches his or her full potential. Although this diversity presents a challenge, it also presents an enormous opportunity to enrich both students' and teachers' lives because of the amazing variety of experiences that can be shared.

However, numerous students, including gifted students, do not experience many of the positive benefits of this diversity. The frequent presence of one-size-fits-all curricula that aim at the "average" student (if one even exists) results in gifted students learning material that they already know. Alternatively, overcrowded classrooms and insufficient professional development can result in teachers who are ill equipped to meet the needs of their students. In addition, pressures from state and federal accountability systems often force teachers to make choices about their time and attention that favor struggling students. As teachers, we have a responsibility to advocate for local, state, and federal policies that will provide smaller classrooms, high-quality professional development, and reasonable accountability systems that do not handicap us from meeting our goal to provide all children with the support they need to flourish and be successful. In the meantime, there are several strategies that can help us work toward that goal.

Instructional Strategies

Compacting the curriculum. Robinson, Shore, and Enersen (2007) estimated that half of general academic content can be removed for gifted learners, with no negative effects on their overall achievement. Curriculum compacting, the practice of teaching gifted students only what they do not already know, depends heavily on accurate preassessment. Without it, teachers will have no way of knowing what their students do and do not know. Preassessment must be closely tied to the learning objectives of the targeted unit of study. In addition, once areas of the curriculum have been removed, it is very important that teachers fill the remaining time with activities designed to challenge gifted learners. A teacher interested in trying curriculum compacting can collaborate with teachers from higher grade levels or a gifted specialist, if available, to plan and implement such learning experiences. A strategy that could be used in conjunction with curriculum compacting—independent studies—is described below.

Independent studies. Independent studies are frequently assigned to gifted students as a means of differentiation. Although they can be an extremely effective tool for providing gifted students with an appropriate degree of challenge and developing lifelong learners, they are often less successful, resulting in misguided, bored, and eventually off-task students. In order for independent studies to become a productive and enjoyable activity in your classroom, it is important to remember that although gifted students may enjoy the independence and freedom granted to them, they still need consistent support and instruction while they are working (Johnsen & Goree, 2005).

Before beginning an independent study with one or more students, you should consider first what skills the students need to be successful. For example, how comfortable are they with independent research, either in books or on the Internet? Organizational skills are also crucial; students may need to keep track of a large amount of information over an extended period of time. Any key skills that students are missing should be introduced before beginning the independent study and monitored throughout the length of the project.

The topic of the independent study may be teacher-directed or student-selected, depending on the overall goals of the project and how it fits in to the rest of the curriculum. There are many models for planning and implementing independent studies; for more information, please see Appendix E.

Conclusion

It is our hope that this book has provided teachers with an overview of the many areas in which verbally gifted students need acceleration, challenge, and support. As teachers of language arts, we must carefully design reading, writing, literature, oral communication, and language instruction that builds on students' verbal talents and addresses their areas of need. Those of us who also teach other subjects can infuse these language arts strategies into those content areas as well. Please remember, however, that implementation of strategies provided by books like this one does not ensure that gifted learners receive the instruction they need. Continuous assessment, reflection, and modification of one's teaching are vital components of good teaching, no matter who the child is. Finally, this book was designed to work in conjunction with many other available resources that explore differentiation techniques for gifted language arts students. Please consult the Resources and References sections for further reading.

Resources

Books

Betts, G. T., & Kercher, J. K. (2001). *The Autonomous Learner Model: Optimizing ability.* Greeley, CO: ALPS
This book is a comprehensive guide to the Autonomous Learner Model, one way of implementing independent studies as part of your instructional program.

Halsted, J. W. (2009). *Some of my best friends are books: Guiding gifted readers* (3rd ed.). Scottsdale, AZ: Great Potential Press. An entire chapter of this book is dedicated to a lengthy annotated bibliography. It includes citations and descriptions of books appropriate for gifted learners. The author organizes the bibliography into five age ranges: preschool, early elementary, upper elementary, middle school, and senior high.

Johnsen, S. K., & Goree, K. (2005). *Independent study for gifted learners.* Waco, TX: Prufrock Press.

This book is a concise guide to planning and implementing independent studies in your classroom and is a great resource for a teacher who is new to the idea and interested in learning more.

Polette, N. J. (2000). *Gifted books, gifted readers: Literature activities to excite young minds.* Englewood, CO: Libraries Unlimited.
This book contains a plethora of classroom activities involving literature that are geared toward gifted students. The author has provided ample suggestions of specific titles that will work for specific needs of gifted learners such as picture books that satisfy the emotional need of coping with stress.

Saul, W., Reardon, J., Pearce, C., Dieckman, D., & Neutze, D. (2002). *Science workshop: Reading, writing, and thinking like a scientist* (2nd ed.). Portsmouth, NH: Heinemann.
This book contains a multitude of strategies and suggestions for infusing literacy instruction into science lessons. Students will learn how to read, write, and think like scientists.

Websites

Books for Advanced Middle Grades Readers
http://mgrn.evansville.edu/vocabulary.htm
This list of books appropriate for gifted middle school students was compiled by a group of library media specialists, classroom teachers, and advanced readers in Indiana.

Books for Children, Featuring Gifted Children
http://www.hoagiesgifted.org/featuring_gifted.htm
This page contains a lengthy list of books that feature characters who are gifted. These books would be a great reference for a teacher looking to use books in bibliotherapy with a gifted reader.

GT–World Reading Lists
http://vcbconsulting.com/gtworld/gtbook.htm
The author of this reading list for gifted readers organized it on a continuum from early picture books through young adult reading rather than assigning grade levels to each section of books.

Armstrong, D. C. (1994). A gifted child's education requires real dialogue: The use of interactive writing for collaborative education. *Gifted Child Quarterly, 38,* 136–145.

Austin, P. (2003). Challenging gifted readers. *Book Links, 12*(5), 32–37.

Bailey, J. M. (1996). Literacy development in verbally talented children. In J. VanTassel-Baska, D. Johnson, & L. N. Boyce (Eds.), *Developing verbal talent: Ideas and strategies for teachers of elementary and middle school students* (pp. 97–114). Boston, MA: Allyn & Bacon.

Bland, L., Coxon, S., Chandler, K., & VanTassel-Baska, J. (2010). Science in the city: Meeting the needs of urban gifted students. *Gifted Child Today, 33*(4), 48–57.

Catron, R. M., & Wingenbach, N. (1986). Developing the potential of the gifted reader. *Theory Into Practice, 25,* 134–140.

Chaney, A. L. (1996). Oral communication: Thinking in action. In J. VanTassel-Baska, D. Johnson, & L. N. Boyce (Eds.), *Developing verbal talent: Ideas and strategies for teachers of elementary and middle school students* (pp. 115–132). Boston, MA: Allyn & Bacon.

Collins, N. D., & Parkhurst, L. (1996). The writing process: A tool for working with gifted students in the regular classroom. *Roeper Review, 18,* 277–280.

Cramond, B. (1993). Speaking and listening: Key components of a complete language arts program for the gifted. *Roeper Review, 16,* 44–48.

Dooley, C. (1993). The challenge: Meeting the needs of gifted readers. *The Reading Teacher, 46,* 546–551.

Duke University Talent Identification Program. (2010). *Characteristics of gifted individuals.* Retrieved from http://www.tip.duke.edu/node/343

Ferguson, R. F. (2003). Teachers' perceptions and expectations and the Black-White test score gap. *Urban Education, 38,* 460–507.

Graves, D. H. (1983). *Writing: Teachers and children at work.* Exeter, NH: Heinemann Educational Books.

Johnsen, S. K., & Goree, K. (2005). *Independent study for gifted learners.* Waco, TX: Prufrock Press.

Kennedy, C. (1996). Teaching discourse through writing. In J. VanTassel-Baska, D. Johnson, & L. N. Boyce (Eds.), *Developing verbal talent: Ideas and strategies for teachers of elementary and middle school students* (pp. 97–114). Boston, MA: Allyn & Bacon.

King, E. W. (2005). Addressing the social and emotional needs of twice-exceptional students. *TEACHING Exceptional Children, 38*(1), 16–20.

Manning, S., & Besnoy, K. D. (2008). Special populations. In F. A. Karnes & K. R. Stephens (Eds.), *Achieving excellence: Educating the gifted and talented* (pp. 116–134). Upper Saddle River, NJ: Pearson.

Master, D. L. (1983). Writing and the gifted child. *Gifted Child Quarterly, 27*(4), 162–168.

Matthews, M. S., & Shaunessy, E. (2008). Culturally, linguistically, and economically diverse gifted students. In F. A.

Karnes & K. R. Stephens (Eds.), *Achieving excellence: educating the gifted and talented* (pp. 99–115). Upper Saddle River, NJ: Pearson.

Olszewski-Kubilius, P., & Thomson, D. (2010). Gifted programming for poor or minority students: Issues and lessons. *Gifted Child Today, 33*(4), 58–64.

Passow, A. H. (1996). Talent identification and development in the language arts. In J. VanTassel-Baska, D. Johnson, & L. N. Boyce (Eds.), *Developing verbal talent: Ideas and strategies for teachers of elementary and middle school students* (pp. 23–33). Boston, MA: Allyn & Bacon.

Piirto, J. (1992). Does writing prodigy exist? How to identify and nurture children with extraordinary writing talent. In N. Colangelo (Ed.), *Talent development: Proceedings from the 1991 Henry B. and Jocelyn Wallace National Research Symposium on Talent Development* (pp. 387–388). Melbourne, Australia: Hawker Brownlow.

Purcell, J. H., Burns, D. E., & Leppien, J. H. (2002). The Parallel Curriculum Model (PCM): The whole story. *Teaching for High Potential, 4*(1), 1–4.

Reis, S. M. (1987). We can't change what we don't recognize: Understanding the special needs of gifted females. *Gifted Child Quarterly, 31,* 83–89.

Reis, S. M., Gubbins, E. J., Briggs, C. J., Schreiber, F. J., Richards, S., Jacobs, J. K., . . . Renzulli, J. S. (2004). Reading instruction for talented readers: Case studies documenting few opportunities for continuous progress. *Gifted Child Quarterly, 48,* 315–338.

Reis, S. M., & Housand, A. M. (2008). Characteristics of gifted and talented learners: Differences and similarities across domains. In F. A. Karnes & K. R. Stephens (Eds.), *Achieving excellence: Educating the gifted and talented* (pp. 62–81). Upper Saddle River, NJ: Pearson.

Rist, R. (1970). Student social class and teacher expectations: The self-fulfilling prophecy in ghetto education. *Harvard Educational Review, 40,* 411–451.

Robinson, A., Shore, B. M., & Enersen, D. L. (2007). *Best practices in gifted education: An evidence-based guide.* Waco, TX: Prufrock Press.

Schunk, D. H., & Swartz, C. W. (1993). Writing strategy instruction with gifted students: Effects of goals and feedback on self-efficacy. *Roeper Review, 15,* 225–230.

Thompson, M. C. (1996a). Formal language study for gifted students. In J. VanTassel-Baska, D. Johnson, & L. N. Boyce (Eds.), *Developing verbal talent: Ideas and strategies for teachers of elementary and middle school students* (pp. 149–173). Boston, MA: Allyn & Bacon.

Thompson, M. C. (1996b). Mentors on paper: How classics develop verbal ability. In J. VanTassel-Baska, D. Johnson, & L. N. Boyce (Eds.), *Developing verbal talent: Ideas and strategies for teachers of elementary and middle school students* (pp. 56–74). Boston, MA: Allyn & Bacon.

Tomlinson, C. A., Kaplan, S. N., Renzulli, J., Purcell, J., Leppien, J., & Burns, D. (2002). *The parallel curriculum: A design to develop high potential and challenge high-ability learners.* Thousand Oaks, CA: Corwin Press.

Weinfeld, R., Barnes-Robinson, L., Jeweler, S., & Shevitz, B. R. (2005). What we have learned: Experiences in providing adaptations and accommodations for gifted and talented students with learning disabilities. *TEACHING Exceptional Children, 38*(1), 48–54.

Wood, P. F. (2008). Reading instruction with gifted and talented readers: A series of unfortunate events or a sequence of auspicious results? *Gifted Child Today, 31*(3), 16–25.

Appendix A

Characteristics of Gifted Students

The following is an excerpted list of characteristics of gifted learners that appears on the Duke University Talent Identification Program's website. Many of the characteristics described below may be found in verbally talented students who may be gifted in the language arts (Duke University Talent Identification Program, 2010).

General Intellectual Ability
- Has varied interests and exhibit curiosity; strong curiosity; asks questions about everything and anything; inquisitive (Clark, 2002; Silverman, 1997–2004; Renzulli, Smith, White, Callahan, Hartman, & Westberg, 2002; Bloom, 1982; Terman & Oden, 1951).
- Demonstrates a high level of language development and verbal ability; has extensive vocabulary; early or avid reader (Clark, 2002; Silverman, 1997–2004; Terman & Oden, 1947; Renzulli, Smith, White, Callahan, Hartman, & Westberg, 2002; Gross, 1993).
- Has an unusual capacity for processing information (Clark, 2002).
- Ability to think and process information quickly; learns rapidly (Clark, 2002; Silverman, 1997–2004).
- Comprehensively synthesizes problems; reasons well (Clark, 2002; Silverman, 1997–2004; Sternberg, 1986).
- Heightened capacity to recognize diverse relationships and integrate ideas across disciplines; reasons things out, comprehends meanings, and makes logical associations. (Renzulli, Smith, White, Callahan, Hartman, & Westberg, 2002).
- Early use of differential patterns in thought processing (Clark, 2002).

- Is a keen observer; alert (Silverman 1997–2004; Renzulli, Smith, White, Callahan, Hartman, & Westberg, 2002; Rogers, 1986; Witty, 1958).

Specific Academic Ability
- Capable of absorbing an extraordinary quantity of information with unusual retentiveness; has an excellent memory (Clark, 2002; Silverman, 1997–2004).
- Able to comprehend subject matter at advanced levels (Clark, 2002).
- Has facility with numbers (Silverman 1997–2004; Gottfried, Gottfried, Bathurst, & Guerin, 1994; Hildreth, 1966; Hollingworth, 1931; Robinson, Roedell, & Jackson, 1979; Rogers, 1986).
- Has quick mastery and recall of factual information; rapid learning ability (Bloom, 1982; Hollingworth, 1942; Terman & Oden, 1947; Renzulli, Smith, White, Callahan, Hartman, & Westberg, 2002).
- Unusual intensity; persistent and goal directed; perseverant in their interests (Clark, 2002; Silverman, 1997–2004; Renzulli, Smith, White, Callahan, Hartman, & Westberg, 2002; Rogers, 1986; Witty, 1958).
- Has a long attention span; perseverant when interested (Feldhusen, 1986; Rogers, 1986; Witty, 1958).

Creative Ability
- Flexible thought processes in solving problems (Clark, 2002).
- Early ability to delay closure (Clark, 2002).
- Can generate original ideas and solutions; is highly creative; offers unusual, unique, or clever answers; originality in written, oral, or artistic expression; independent thinker (Clark, 2002; Silverman, 1997–2004; Renzulli, Smith, White, Callahan, Hartman, & Westberg, 2002; Lovecky, 1993; Rogers, 1986).

- Has a vivid imagination; fantasizes (Silverman 1997–2004; J. Gallagher, 1966; S. Gallagher, 1985; Piechowski & Colangelo, 1984; Piechowski, Silverman, & Falk, 1985; Terman & Oden, 1959; Renzulli, Smith, White, Callahan, Hartman, & Westberg, 2002).
- Has a keen sense of humor; comical (Silverman, 1997–2004; Renzulli, Smith, White, Callahan, Hartman, & Westberg, 2002; Hollingworth, 1926; Terman, 1925; Kanevsky, Maker, Nielsen, & Rogers, 1994).
- Is a risk-taker; adventurous and speculative (Renzulli, Smith, White, Callahan, Hartman, & Westberg, 2002).
- Involvement with the metaneeds of society (beauty, justice, truth); is sensitive to beauty (Clark, 2002; Renzulli, Smith, White, Callahan, Hartman, & Westberg, 2002).
- Nonconforming; individualistic (Renzulli, Smith, White, Callahan, Hartman, & Westberg, 2002).
- Uses previously learned things in new contexts (Smutny, 1998).

References

Bloom, B. S. (1982). The role of gifts and markers in the development of talent. *Exceptional Children, 48,* 510–521.

Clark, B. (2002). *Growing up gifted* (5th ed.) Columbus, OH: Charles E. Merrill.

Feldhusen, J. F. (1986). A conception of giftedness. In R. J. Sternberg & J. E. Davidson (Eds.), *Conceptions of giftedness* (pp. 112–127). Cambridge, MA: Cambridge University Press.

Gallagher, J. J. (1966). *Research summary on gifted child education.* Springfield, IL: Office of the Illinois Superintendent of Public Instruction.

Gallagher, S. A. (1985). A comparison of the concept of over-excitabilities with measures of creativity and school achievement in sixth grade students. *Roeper Review, 8,* 115–119.

Gross, M. U. M. (1993). *Exceptionally gifted children.* London, England: Routledge.

Hollingworth, L. S. (1926). *Gifted children: Their nature and nurture.* New York, NY: Macmillan.

Hollingworth, L. S. (1931). The child of very superior intelligence as a special problem in social adjustment. *Mental Hygiene, 15*(1), 1–16.

Hollingworth, L. S. (1942). *Children above 180 IQ Stanford-Binet: Origin and development.* Yonkers-on-Hudson, NY: World Book.

Kanevsky, L., Maker, C. J., Nielsen, A., & Rogers, K. B. (1994). Brilliant behaviors. In C. J. Maker & A. Nielsen, *Principles and curriculum development for the gifted.* Austin, TX: Pro-Ed.

Lovecky, D. V. (1993). The quest for meaning: Counseling issues with gifted children and adolescents. In L. K. Silverman (Ed.), *Counseling the gifted and talented* (pp. 29–50). Denver, CO: Love.

Piechowski, M. M., & Colangelo, N. (1984). Developmental potential of the gifted. *Gifted Child Quarterly, 28,* 80–88.

Piechowski, M. M., Silverman, L. K., & Falk, R. F. (1985). Comparison of intellectually and artistically gifted on five dimensions of mental functioning. *Perceptual and Motor Skills, 60,* 539–549.

Renzulli, J. S., Smith, L. H., White, A. J., Callahan, C. M., Hartman, R. K., & Westberg, K. L. (2002). *Scales for rating the behavioral characteristics of superior students* (Rev. ed.). Mansfield Center, CT: Creative Learning Press.

Robinson, H. B., Roedell, W. C., & Jackson, N. E. (1979). Early identification and intervention. In A. H. Passow (Ed.), *The gifted and talented: Their education and development* (pp. 138–154). The 78th yearbook of the National Society for the Study of Education, Part I. Chicago, IL: The University of Chicago Press.

Rogers, M. T. (1986). *A comparative study of developmental traits of gifted and average children.* Unpublished doctoral dissertation, University of Denver, Denver, CO.

Silverman, L. K. (1997–2004). *Characteristics of giftedness scale: A review of the literature.* Retrieved April 25, 2005 from www. gifteddevelopment.com

Smutny, J. F. (Ed.). (1998). *The young gifted child: Potential and promise, an anthology.* Cresskill, NJ: Hampton Press.

Sternberg, R. J. (1986). A triarchic theory of intellectual giftedness. In R. J. Sternberg & J. E. Davidson (Eds.), *Conceptions of giftedness* (pp. 223–243). Cambridge, MA: Cambridge University Press.

Terman, L. M. (1925). *Genetic studies of genius: Vol. 1. Mental and physical traits of a thousand gifted children.* Stanford, CA: Stanford University Press.

Terman, L. M., & Oden, M. H. (1947). *Genetic studies of genius: Vol. 4. The gifted child grows up.* Stanford, CA: Stanford University Press.

Terman, L. M., & Oden, M. H. (1951). The Stanford studies of the gifted. In P. Witty (Ed.), *The gifted child* (pp. 20–46). Boston, MA: D. C. Heath.

Terman, L. M., & Oden, M. H. (1959). *Genetic studies of genius: Vol. 5. The gifted group at mid-life.* Stanford, CA: Stanford University Press.

Witty, P. A. (1958). Who are the gifted? In N. B. Henry (Ed.), *Education for the gifted* (pp. 42–63). The fifty-seventh yearbook of the National Society for the Study of Education, Part II. Chicago, IL: The University of Chicago Press.

Note. The excerpt in Appendix A was reprinted with permission from Duke University Talent Identification Program.

Appendix B

Paideia Seminars

A Paideia Seminar is a moderated discussion based on a text that is guided through open-ended questioning. The following lesson plan is a Paideia Seminar designed for students in grades 2–4. There are several elements of this lesson that meet the needs of gifted learners, although the lesson is designed for a heterogeneous classroom. First of all, the questions are open-ended and higher level, which engages students in critical thinking. The literature is authentic and historic, which adds another dimension of meaning for gifted readers. Finally, the lesson combines several aspects of language arts development, including reading, listening, and speaking. By adding overt practice with oral communication skills, gifted learners are able to build their ability to think quickly, practice using evidence to justify conclusions, and critically listen to the ideas of others.

Unit: Fairy Tales and Folk Tales Around the World
Text: "Anansi and Turtle"
Author: Tshi-speaking people of Africa, retold by Mary Furlough

Opening Question:
- Who is cleverer, Anansi or Turtle? (round-robin)

Focus Questions:
- Did Turtle know Anansi was tricking him? (Or, did Anansi know Turtle was tricking him?) How do you know?
- Was Anansi wrong to trick Turtle? (Or, was Turtle wrong to trick Anansi?) Why do you think so?
- In many Anansi stories, he is portrayed as greedy. Is being greedy a bad quality? Is every person greedy to an extent?
- How are the customs of this community in Africa the same as or different from our customs?

- Are everyone's customs in our community the same? What are some customs of hospitality your family follows?

Closing Question:
- Tell about a time you have not wanted to share something of yours with someone else. What did you do?
- Are you greedy or generous? (round-robin)

What Is the "Great Idea" of This Piece?
- You reap what you sow.

Appendix C

Concept-Based Lesson Plan

Concept Development, Early Elementary

This lesson is designed to occur in the early stages of a concept-based instructional unit focusing on the concept of family, during which students are exploring their initial understandings of the concept. In this particular lesson, students are beginning to think about the universal nature of families as well as the similarities and differences between different families. The process of concept development has four main steps: brainstorming examples, categorizing examples, brainstorming nonexamples, and developing generalizations. This process serves as the foundation of the unit; basing your instruction on the students' initial understandings will help to increase their engagement and enthusiasm for the topic. Gifted students will enjoy thinking about a very common idea in a deeper and more abstract way.

This lesson is easily adaptable for different grade levels, mainly in the degree of teacher involvement. Although each group of students is different, in general, younger students will probably need more teacher modeling and support than older students. Older students may be able to work in small groups while the teacher monitors. This lesson can be spread out over multiple days, and different activities can be inserted to check students' understanding and assess their progress. For example, students can respond to questions in writing or orally.

Activities and Guiding Questions

Students will participate in a guided visualization activity by closing their eyes and thinking about the following prompts:
- Think about the word *family*.
- What people do you see? Do you see your family?
- What about other families? What are they doing?

Concept Development Step 1: Brainstorming Examples

Students will work as a group to make a list of as many words/phrases that they can think of that relate the word *family*. Responses will be recorded on chart paper. The following questions and prompts can be used to guide and expand students' thinking:

- What words come to mind?
- Who has a family?
- Who makes up a family?
- What does a family do?
- What is a family like?
- A family is . . .

Concept Development Step 2: Categories Development

After making an expansive list, the students' next task is to put their ideas into groups in order to think more carefully about the words and ideas they have collected. If necessary, the teacher can model this process by naming the first group, "people in families," and picking one item that belongs in that group (e.g., Mom) and deciding against an item that does not belong (e.g., eating dinner together). Additional possibilities for categories include:

- Things families do
- Describing words
- Different kinds of families

Student thinking should guide the categorization process as much as possible, with the teacher modeling and scaffolding as necessary.

Concept Development Step 3: Listing Nonexamples

Next, students will brainstorm things that are not in a family so that they can begin to understand what is important and unique about families. The following questions and prompts can be used to guide students thinking about nonexamples:

- What is not in a family?

- A family is not . . .
- A family does not . . .

Concept Development Step 4: Generalize

The final step of initial concept development is for students to come up with generalizations about the concept, which will be subject to revision as their understandings change and develop over the course of the unit. If necessary, the teacher can model this process by thinking aloud about one of the groups that was brainstormed (e.g., "people in families") and coming up with a generalization for that group with student input.

Students will work in groups to come up with a few key generalizations. These will be recorded on a concept map for the word family. Possible generalizations include:

- Families are _____ because _____.
- Families are different because _____.
- Families are the same because _____.
- Different families have differences and things in commons.
- Lots of different people can make up a family.
- All living things are part of a family.

Appendix D

Ideas and Activities for Writing in the Content Areas

Math

Writing is integrated in math instruction probably the least out of any subject area, but using writing in math can greatly enhance math instruction. Writing can be used to help students:

- Reflect
  - o Write about what you did in class today.
  - o What did you learn?
  - o What are you unsure about, confused by, or wondering about?
  - o Describe what was easy and what was hard for you.
- Explain
  - o How are multiplication and division alike and different?
  - o Explain what _____ (e.g., multiplication, division, the number 5) means in your own words.
- Summarize
  - o Solve the following problem and write a summary of the steps you took to solve it.

Social Studies

Writing in a variety of genres can be used to immerse students in study of historical events. For example, in a study of explorers of North America, students can:

- write newspaper articles with interviews of famous explorers,
- prepare brochures encouraging people to travel to the New World,
- write letters describing challenges of colonial life, and
- create posters advertising town meetings.

Science

Science notebooks or journals are a great way to incorporate writing into your science instruction. As you plan your students' use of science journals, you may want to consider the following questions.

- Organization: Teachers should guide students as they develop organizational skills, but students should be able to organize material in ways that make sense to them.
  - o Questions to consider:
    - Do students start each new entry on a blank page or continue from the day before?
    - Will notebooks be divided into different sections?
    - Idea: Fold over right margin to leave space for notes, answers to questions, new questions, comments on observations, and the like.
- Purpose: If students are not made aware of and invested in the purpose of their notebooks, the practice of writing loses its meaning and becomes busy work.
  - o Possible purposes:
    - Create/organize scientific findings to share with a larger audience.
    - Record thoughts/ideas to contribute to daily discussions.
    - Have a personal/internal sounding board.
- Content: Content may be set by state/district curricular goals. The level of student choice/input depends on instructional model and level of inquiry
  - o Questions to consider:
    - What are students studying?
    - What kinds of thoughts/ideas do I want students to record?

- What level of structure will I provide (e.g., free response, response to prompts/questions, teacher-set topic)?
    - What level of student choice seems appropriate?
- Process Skills: If content is the "what," process skills are the "how":
    o The emphasis of certain process skills depends on focus and goals of the science unit.
    o Process skills include observing, communicating, measuring, comparing, contrasting, organizing, classifying, analyzing, and so forth.
- Mode of Representation: How students will record their thoughts and ideas?
    o Questions to consider:
        - Do students have to use words? Can pictures be used?
        - Do I want students to label pictures with a caption?
        - Will students use tables, charts, and graphs?

Writing-to-Learn Activities

Shorter, more informal writing tasks that are designed to help students develop critical thinking skills and think through key concepts and ideas include:
- List-Group-Label
    o Students work in a group to make a list of important words pertaining to a certain topic.
    o Students group words together that have similar characteristics.
    o Students label their groups.
    o Students explain their thinking to the rest of the class or summarize their group's thinking in writing.

- Microthemes
  o Students respond to a prompt or question on a small index card.
- Strip Stories
  o Students participate in an activity (e.g., watching a video clip, researching online, reading one or more texts).
  o Students retell and sequence the important elements of the activity in a finite number or boxes.

Appendix E

Independent Study

The following is an independent study guide that could be used with verbally talented elementary students. Because an independent study is inherently self-directed by the student, this plan is not meant as an exact blueprint but instead is intended to guide the student in meeting the teacher's expectations. Students who are uncomfortable with ambiguity or have difficulty with organization or self-directed tasks will need more teacher guidance and support.

Unit: Fairy Tales
Grade: Elementary
Objective: Student(s) will be able to change elements of a fairy tale (e.g., plot, setting, characters, point of view) to create their own fractured fairy tale.

Preassess students on their knowledge of story elements. Students with extensive knowledge of story elements should be omitted from further study and allowed to pursue this independent study. Students who work on this lesson will need some prior experience with fairy tales.

- Read students some fractured fairy tales such as *The True Story of the Three Little Pigs*, *The Princess and the Pizza*, *The Wolf Who Cried Boy*, and *The Stinky Cheese Man*.
- Students will then complete the following steps:
  o Think about the fairy tales we have read in class or some of your favorite tales you have read on your own or with your family. Choose one story that you will turn into your own fractured fairy tale. Why did you choose this story?
  o List the important elements of the familiar story. Brainstorm ways you could change these elements by filling out the chart below.

Story Elements	Fairy Tale	Fractured Fairy Tale
Setting		
Good Characters		
Evil Characters		
Point of View		
Problem		
Solution		

- o Create a rubric to be used in grading your story. Here are some categories you might consider: spelling and grammar, descriptive language, creativity, and use of story elements.
- o Use your chart to write your story. Remember to keep the same general outline of the original fairy tale, changing the story elements to make it fractured.
- o When you are finished with your story, remember to read it twice and fill out the editor's checklist. Ask a classmate to read it twice and fill out another editor's checklist.
- o Meet with your teacher to edit your story one last time. Fill out your rubric with the help of your teacher.
- o Publish your story. You may use Microsoft Word to type your story and do illustrations by hand or use Kid Pix. If you have another idea for a way to publish your story, ask your teacher.
- o Choose an audience for your story. Some possible choices include another class in our school, a class at a different school, a preschool class, or a library story hour. Read your story to the audience you choose.

Lauren Miller is a Nationally Board Certified elementary teacher who lives and works in Durham, NC. She studied gifted education at Duke University, where she also earned her bachelor's degree. She holds a master's degree in curriculum and instruction from North Carolina State University. Her research interests are rooted in teacher education, particularly in preparing teachers to meet the needs of academically diverse learners in heterogeneous classrooms.

Emily Lubkert is an elementary teacher who has worked in New York City and Chicago. She has studied gifted education from Duke University, where she also completed her undergraduate studies. She holds a master's degree in instructional leadership from the Harvard Graduate School of Education, where she focused on urban education, teacher leadership, and instructional improvement through teacher collaboration.

Printed in the United States
by Baker & Taylor Publisher Services